AF413527

# CAN I BUILD SANDCASTLES ON A SNOWY DAY?

## WEATHER WORKBOOKS FOR KIDS

### Children's Weather Books

Let's have fun learning about the weather!

hello
Spring

During spring you get a lot of sunshine. Plants begin to bloom and animals come out of hibernation to enjoy the warmth after a cold winter.

SUMMER

During summer it gets hotter. This is a great time to spend outdoors at the beach or pool to keep cool.

A lot of weather cases tends to happen this time of year such as storms.

Tornado

Thunderstorm

AUTUMN

During autumn it gets cooler and sometimes windy. The leaves on trees begin to change color to golds, rust red, orange and brown. Also it may begin to rain a lot.

WINTER

During winter it is cold. It begins to snow in some regions and persons would have to dress very warm if they are going outside.

# LET'S DO SOME FUN ACTIVITIES

# YOUR TASK

USE THE FIRST LETTER OF EACH
PICTURE BELOW THE BOXES TO
SOLVE THE WORD

# YOUR TASK

COMPLETE THE WORDS

r

S

W

W

C

f

S

| t |  |  |  |  |  |  |
|---|---|---|---|---|---|---|

o

# YOUR TASK

THIS IS A ZIGZAG WORD SEARCH PUZZLE.
WORDS GO LEFT, RIGHT, UP, DOWN, NOT
DIAGONALLY AND CAN BEND AT A RIGHT
ANGLE. THERE ARE NO UNUSED LETTERS
IN THE GRID, EVERY LETTER IS USED ONLY
ONCE.


FIND ALL THE WORDS FROM THE WORD LIST
(IGNORE SPACES AND DASHES, IF ANY)

# Weather

| C | S | N | O | W | C | L | O | U | M |
|---|---|---|---|---|---|---|---|---|---|
| A | K | A | L | F | D | E | W | D | I |
| L | E | G | B | H | A | I | L | W | S |
| M | L | N | L | R | S | Q | R | O | T |
| C | I | I | I | A | I | U | A | B | S |
| L | G | N | Z | Z | N | A | I | N | N |
| E | H | T | F | A | L | L | E | R | O |
| A | R | F | R | R | D | D | D | S | W |
| M | O | O | O | W | I | N | N | T | M |
| S | G | G | S | T | T | H | U | O | R |

| | | | |
|---|---|---|---|
| BLIZZARD | DEW | MIST | SNOWFLAKE |
| CALM | FOG | RAIN | SQUALL |
| CLEAR | FROST | RAINBOW | THUNDERSTORM |
| CLOUD | HAIL | SMOG | WIND |
| | LIGHTNING | SNOW | |

# Spring

| APRIL | GARDEN | SEEDS |
|---|---|---|
| BIRDHOUSE | GREEN GRASS | SOWING |
| BLOSSOM | MARCH | SUNLIGHT |
| BLUE SKY | MAY | YOUNG GROWTH |
| FRESHNESS | NESTLINGS | |

# Summer

| | | | | | | | | | |
|---|---|---|---|---|---|---|---|---|---|
| H | O | T | G | S | U | N | H | F | T |
| N | E | E | R | Y | E | N | O | R | I |
| G | R | A | S | S | I | D | S | E | U |
| H | A | L | O | F | M | Y | U | S | R |
| O | U | I | E | J | U | L | M | H | F |
| L | G | A | G | B | R | E | M | V | A |
| I | U | W | I | U | T | T | E | R | C |
| D | S | T | L | B | E | Y | L | F | A |
| A | Y | S | D | F | E | N | O | I | T |
| E | N | U | J | L | O | W | E | R | S |

AUGUST  GREEN GRASS  JUNE

BEE  HOLIDAYS  MIDSUMMER

BUTTERFLY  HONEY  SUN

FOLIAGE  HOT  VACATION

FRESH FRUIT  JULY  WILDFLOWERS

# Autumn

| P | U | D | S | R | V | T | O | S | C |
|---|---|---|---|---|---|---|---|---|---|
| E | L | D | E | A | E | K | E | M | H |
| O | E | R | P | H | S | C | V | B | O |
| C | B | R | T | R | T | A | O | E | O |
| T | O | E | E | A | I | B | N | R | L |
| R | S | B | M | N | N | F | A | L | L |
| U | E | A | S | O | E | L | G | N | I |
| B | H | A | L | L | A | V | E | S | C |
| B | S | T | O | O | W | E | E | N | O |
| E | R | B | O | E | Z | A | M | N | R |

BACK TO SCHOOL   HARVEST   RAIN

CORN MAZE   NOVEMBER   RUBBER BOOTS

FALLING LEAVES   OCTOBER   SEASON

HALLOWEEN   PUDDLE   SEPTEMBER

# Winter

| B | D | E | T | S | O | R | F | S | C |
|---|---|---|---|---|---|---|---|---|---|
| A | S | C | N | E | W | Y | F | R | A |
| R | E | E | J | R | A | E | M | I | T |
| E | E | M | A | S | N | O | W | M | T |
| T | R | B | N | U | A | S | N | A | E |
| I | T | E | I | S | R | N | E | I | N |
| N | A | R | C | K | Y | O | L | C | S |
| G | K | S | E | I | F | W | C | I | H |
| F | E | B | R | I | L | A | S | L | G |
| Y | R | A | U | N | G | K | E | E | I |

| BARE TREES | ICICLE | SKIING |
|---|---|---|
| DECEMBER | JANUARY | SLEIGH |
| FEBRUARY | MITTENS | SNOWFLAKE |
| FROST | NEW YEAR | SNOWMAN |
| ICE SKATING | SCARF | |

# ANSWERS

**1.** 

**umbrella**

**2.** 

**Rain**

# 3. Snowfall

# 4. Cloud

# Day

**6.**

| r | a | i | n |
|---|---|---|---|

**7.**

| s | u | n |
|---|---|---|

8.

snowfall

**9.**

w | i | n | d

**10.**

c | l | o | u | d | y

**11.**

| s | t | o | r | m |
|---|---|---|---|---|

**12.**

| s | n | o | w | f | l | a | k | e |
|---|---|---|---|---|---|---|---|---|

| t | o | r | n | a | d | o |
|---|---|---|---|---|---|---|

14.

| r | a | i | n | b | o | w |

# 15. Weather

# 16. Spring

# 17. Summer

## 18. Autumn

| P | U | D | S | R | V | T | O | S | C |
| E | L | D | E | A | E | K | E | M | H |
| O | E | R | P | H | S | C | V | B | O |
| C | B | R | T | R | T | A | O | E | O |
| T | O | E | E | A | I | B | N | R | L |
| R | S | B | M | N | N | F | A | L | L |
| U | E | A | S | O | E | L | G | N | I |
| B | H | A | L | L | A | V | E | S | C |
| B | S | T | O | O | W | E | E | N | O |
| E | R | B | O | E | Z | A | M | N | R |

## 19. Winter

| B | D | E | T | S | O | R | F | S | C |
| A | S | C | N | E | W | Y | F | R | A |
| R | E | E | J | R | A | E | M | I | T |
| E | E | M | A | S | N | O | W | M | T |
| T | R | B | N | U | A | S | N | A | E |
| I | T | E | I | S | R | N | E | I | N |
| N | A | R | C | K | Y | O | L | C | S |
| G | K | S | E | I | F | W | C | I | H |
| F | E | B | R | I | L | A | S | L | G |
| Y | R | A | U | N | G | K | E | E | I |

Visit
BABY PROFESSOR
EDUCATION KIDS
www.BabyProfessorBooks.com
to download Free Baby Professor eBooks
and view our catalog of new and exciting
Children's Books